IMAGES
of America

FORT
SAM HOUSTON

D1608955

John Manguso

ARCADIA
PUBLISHING

Published by Arcadia Publishing
Charleston, South Carolina

Printed in the United States of America

Library of Congress Control Number: 2012944287

For all general information, please contact Arcadia Publishing:
Telephone 843-853-2070
Fax 843-853-0044
E-mail sales@arcadiapublishing.com
For customer service and orders:
Toll-Free 1-888-313-2665

Visit us on the Internet at www.arcadiapublishing.com

This book is dedicated to all those who have had the wisdom and courage to participate in the defense of the United States of America.

CONTENTS

ACKNOWLEDGMENTS

The images in this volume appear courtesy of the Fort Sam Houston Museum and the Library of Congress Historic American Building Survey (HABS). Unless otherwise noted, images are from the collections of the Fort Sam Houston Museum. For its help in providing the majority of the images in this book, I thank the staff of the Fort Sam Houston Museum. These photographs represent only a tiny fraction of the museum's rich photograph collections.

I would like to thank the following people: Mrs. Dunmire, my first history teacher, for getting me interested in history; Dr. John K. Mahon, my advisor in graduate school at the University of Florida; Brig. Gen. Joseph P. Kingston, who gave me my job as military history detachment commander; Maj. Gen. Henry Mohr, chief of the Army Reserve, who advised me to "tell it like it is, even if no one believes you;" Maj. Bennie Boles, who hired me as a museum curator at Fort Sam Houston; Col. Jim O'Neal, Ed Miller, and Ron Still, three of the best supervisors a museum director could have; Joan Gaither, whose support as president of Preservation Fort Sam Houston has been invaluable; and Laura Bruns, my editor at Arcadia Publishing, who provided support and guidance throughout the preparation of this book.

Special thanks go to Jacqueline Davis, who has been my strong right arm for most of the 33 years I spent at the Fort Sam Houston Museum. Most of all, I thank my beloved wife of 45 years, Barbara, whose support has been . . . priceless.

INTRODUCTION

Nestled within the city limits of San Antonio, Texas, is Fort Sam Houston. This 3,000-acre military reservation is home to the largest and most sophisticated military medical education and training institution in the world, the Military Education and Training Campus. It is also home to the headquarters of Army North and Army South, the Army Medical Command, Joint Base San Antonio, and the Army Installation Management Command. Through these organizations, Fort Sam Houston exerts a worldwide influence in the defense of the United States. But it was not always thus.

Fort Sam Houston became San Antonio's Army post in 1845, when the 2nd Regiment of Dragoons arrived in town and established the post at San Antonio. The mission of the post was to secure the border with Mexico and to protect the residents of Texas from hostile Indians. In all, five missions would be performed there: headquarters, garrison, logistical base, mobilization and training site, and medical facility. Throughout its history, these five missions shaped the development of Fort Sam Houston. In its first decade in town, the Army established a small garrison, a regional headquarters, a supply depot, and a hospital. However, there was no installation; all activities were conducted from rented buildings in the city, including the Alamo.

The post at San Antonio was surrendered to rebel forces in February 1861 as the Civil War split the nation. In 1865, Union forces returned and resumed operations as before. Due to the high cost of rent in town, the Army considered closing the post and moving elsewhere. To keep the post in town, the city council offered 92 acres of land for a permanent post on what became known as Government Hill. The offer was accepted, and construction began in 1876 on the Quartermaster Depot. In 1878, the depot building was expanded for the Headquarters, Department of Texas, but the lack of officer quarters kept the headquarters in town. The garrison moved into tents and temporary buildings west of the depot in 1879. In 1881, when officer quarters were built on the Lower Post, the headquarters moved into the depot.

Land was purchased in 1882 east of the depot to accommodate those facilities still in town. Between 1885 and 1894, barracks, a post headquarters, officer quarters, noncommissioned officer quarters, a band barracks, a guardhouse, and an officers' mess were constructed here. The post was then the second largest Army post in the United States. It was fitting, then, that the Army designated the post as Fort Sam Houston in 1890.

In 1898, as the United States mobilized for war with Spain, the garrison of the post shipped out for service overseas. The 1st US Volunteer Cavalry, known as Roosevelt's Rough Riders, mobilized in San Antonio. After the war, the Army expanded, and so did Fort Sam Houston. Construction began in 1905 on barracks, officer quarters, noncommissioned officer quarters, a guardhouse, a bakery, and a station hospital. Completion of this, the Cavalry and Light Artillery Post Addition, permitted the billeting of the garrison in complete units within the same neighborhood. The Upper Post became the Infantry Post and the Lower Post became the Staff Post. It also made Fort Sam Houston America's largest Army post.

Fort Sam Houston became the testing ground for the Army's only aircraft in 1910 as the Signal Corps tried to figure out what the contraption could be used for. When turbulence along the border with Mexico brewed, a maneuver division was assembled here "just in case." After Pancho Villa's raid on Columbus, New Mexico, Brig. Gen. John Pershing led a punitive expedition into Mexico. Regular Army units were relocated to the border area, and 100,000 National Guardsmen were mobilized for service. The Southern Department Headquarters in the Quadrangle commanded the forces on the border from Brownsville to the California state line and the punitive expedition. To supply this force, the depot leased storage space in San Antonio.

The punitive expedition was withdrawn in 1917 as the United States entered World War I. Fort Sam Houston experienced a frantic expansion as mobilization began. Construction was begun on Camp Travis, a cantonment with a capacity for 50,000 soldiers. It was completed in 90 days, in time for the arrival of the first draftees. During the war, more than 120,000 doughboys passed through Camp Travis. After the war, the 2nd Division was assigned to Fort Sam Houston.

In the reduction of the Army after the "war to end all wars," upkeep of the temporary buildings was cut, and their condition deteriorated. The peacetime routine was such that the War Department lent the troops at Fort Sam Houston to the motion picture industry for three major films: *The Rough Riders*, *The Big Parade*, and *Wings*. The living conditions for the soldiers at Fort Sam Houston and elsewhere were awful, and replacement of the temporary buildings was necessary.

In 1926, Congress enacted the Army Housing Program, providing well-designed communities for the nation's military posts. At Fort Sam Houston, this resulted in construction of the New Post and the introduction of the Spanish Colonial Revival style of architecture.

As Fort Sam Houston was the only post with a division garrison, the Army called upon it to test new tactical concepts. In field exercises between 1937 and 1941, the 2nd Division developed the Triangular Division, a mobile and powerful organization for modern war. The 2nd Division also experimented with airborne operations.

During the lead-up to World War II, Fort Sam Houston units participated in large-scale maneuvers in Louisiana. After Pearl Harbor, the post became a beehive of activity. Three infantry divisions and a host of smaller units—Quartermaster Corps, Signal Corps, Railway Operations, Ordnance, Medical Corps, Military Police, and Chemical Corps—trained and deployed overseas. By the end of World War II, more than one million Americans had passed through Fort Sam Houston.

After the war, the Army sought a new role for Fort Sam Houston because it was no longer large enough for the training of a division. In 1947, the Medical Field Service School was transferred here, putting the post on the path to become the "home of Army medicine." The other missions remained the same, with the Fourth Army Headquarters in the Quadrangle commanding all the units and installations in Texas, Arkansas, Louisiana, Oklahoma, and New Mexico.

During the Korean War, the Vietnam War, and the Cold War, medical activities continued to grow. In 1975, Fort Sam Houston's long service and contributions to the nation were recognized in its designation as a National Historic Landmark. After 1975, Fort Sam Houston would see more change, but its five basic missions remained the same.

Throughout its history, Fort Sam Houston has been one of this nation's most important military installations. From its origins in 1845 in rented buildings in San Antonio, the post at San Antonio has developed into Fort Sam Houston, the "home of military medicine." Despite the growth and change, Fort Sam Houston has retained the sense of its past. The fort's soldiers live, work, and train where more than a million soldiers, sailors, airmen, and marines have served. Through careful preservation, Fort Sam Houston keeps the spirit and values of the Army alive as it continues to serve the nation.

One

THE POST ON
GOVERNMENT HILL
1870–1898

Construction of a building for the Quartermaster Depot on Government Hill began on June 21, 1876. By August 12, the layout of the walls of the Quartermaster Depot was apparent, and construction had begun on the water tower. The building enclosed a courtyard of 8.5 acres and had more than one acre of indoor storage space.

In this 1877 view, the blacksmith and wheelwright shops along the north wall were still under construction, while the 90-foot-tall tower had just been completed. The tower was originally built to hold a 70,000-gallon water tank and to provide a station for a watchman at the 60-foot level, which takes 103 steps to get to.

Along the inner side of the north wall of the Quadrangle were the blacksmith and wheelwright shops. Here, a blacksmith stands by one of the four forges with an array of tools. Assorted wagon parts and wheels are in the shop undergoing repairs. This shop was also where the horses and mules were shoed.

When construction of the depot was completed in 1877, the first floor of the southern side was occupied by storerooms. In the center was a sally port for entering into the courtyard. Inside the sally port was a stairwell leading to the second story. On the second story, above the center third of the building, were the offices for the Quartermaster Depot staff.

Between 1877 and 1879, the second-story center section of the depot was extended to the full length of the building to provide additional office space. This was intended for the commanding general and staff of the Headquarters, Department of Texas, which were still located in rented buildings in San Antonio.

11

The eastern end of the expanded second story of the Quadrangle, with its arcade, is seen here. Though the expansion was completed in 1879, the headquarters did not move in until 1881, because there were no quarters on the post for the commanding general and his staff. Until there were quarters, the general and his staff lived and worked in San Antonio.

Brig. Gen. David S. Stanley, the commander of the Department of Texas and a Medal of Honor recipient for heroism during the Civil War, sits at his desk in the Quadrangle. His tenure as commander from 1884 to 1892 was the longest of any officer to command from the Quadrangle.

In September 1886, the Apache war chief Geronimo was held prisoner in the Quadrangle. He and the other Apaches were en route to imprisonment in Florida. There is no evidence to support the legends that he jumped from the tower or that the deer in the Quadrangle were put there to feed the Apaches.

In this view from the north side of the Quadrangle looking south, the extension of the second-story center section to the full length of the building is visible. The tower does not yet have a clock face on the north side. At the far left, part of the roof of the bachelor officer quarters is visible, dating this photograph to around 1895.

Maj. Peter Vroom, formerly of the 3rd Cavalry, served as the inspector general of the Department of Texas from 1888 to 1895. He sits here in a buggy in front of the building that housed the department headquarters and the Quartermaster Depot. The original image identifies the two horses but not the three ladies in the picture. Major Vroom would later become the inspector general of the Army.

In 1881, Alfred Giles designed 15 sets of officer quarters that were built west of the Quadrangle. This view from the clock tower around 1890 shows the Lower Post parade ground and all of the quarters. The commanding general's quarters, flanked by two company-grade quarters for his aides-de-camp, can be seen at the bend in the road.

Brig. Gen. David S. Stanley, in the white coat and dark trousers, and Anna Stanley, in the dark dress, sit with three of their four daughters and three unidentified guests in the front yard of their quarters on the Lower Post. The two uniformed officers behind Stanley are his aides-de-camp. Three of General Stanley's daughters would marry his aides-de-camp.

Assignment of quarters on the Lower Post depended on the rank and duty assignment of the occupant. The quarters on the left were company-grade—captain or lieutenant—quarters designated for one of the aides-de-camp of the commanding general, as they were next door to the commander's quarters. On the right is one of the field-grade—major, lieutenant colonel, or colonel—quarters.

Capt. Oskaloosa M. Smith (left), aide-de-camp to General Stanley, and Capt. James G. Ballance, judge advocate for the Department of Texas, sit in the front yard of their quarters on the Lower Post in July 1886. Though these quarters were built for married field-grade officers, the Army often billeted multiple bachelor officers in them.

Capt. Oskaloosa M. Smith and three other unidentified people look as though they are going out for a picnic. Another woman, probably a servant, looks on from the front porch of the quarters. Captain Smith's hat is strictly non-regulation. In the background is one of the quarters designated for the commanding general's aides-de-camp.

In 1886, a 12-bed hospital was constructed in the center of the line of officer quarters on the Lower Post. As newer medical facilities on the post were built, this building was used as a dental clinic, a barracks, and for office space before becoming the distinguished visitor quarters in 1951. Though Sam Houston never lived there, the building was designated as the Sam Houston House in 1961.

Members of the Hospital Corps assemble behind the post hospital for a group photograph. They are wearing the five-button blouse with the 1895-pattern garrison cap. Hospital stewards can be identified by a wreath around the cross on their caps. Prior to the establishment of the Hospital Corps in 1887, enlisted men detailed from the line units assisted the surgeons in the hospitals and served as litter bearers.

Brig. Gen. Frank Wheaton, seated front and center, poses with the staff of the Headquarters, Department of Texas, at his quarters on the Lower Post on April 11, 1894. These officers are wearing their full dress uniforms. Standing at the far left is Maj. Arthur MacArthur, a Medal of Honor recipient and the father of Gen. Douglas MacArthur, who would also receive the Medal of Honor.

Oskaloosa Minnewando Smith wears his dress uniform as a first lieutenant of the 22nd Infantry. The spacing of the buttons on the coat and the rows of braid on his belt identify him as a company-grade officer. The aiguillette on his right shoulder indicates he is detailed as an aide-de-camp to a general officer—in this case to Brigadier General Stanley.

In 1892, this gun shed was built to park the equipment of the light artillery battery stationed on the post. The building would hold four cannons, four ammunition caissons, and four limbers. The room at the right end of the building was for the storage of saddles, harnesses, and other section equipment.

Outside the artillery gun shed next to the Quadrangle stands Pvt. ? Sanders and his horse, Dude. Private Sanders is armed with the Pattern of 1840 Light Artillery Saber and a Colt revolver. Dude is equipped with the M1885 McClellan artillery saddle. Behind him, the gun shed stores the equipment of Light Battery F, 3rd Artillery.

A 17867 Soldiers Quarters (Portion of 1602), San Antonio, Tex.

Ft. Sam Houston has a new addition to the north. Isn't this a pretty sight? From Helen

The 23-acre parade ground on the Upper Post provided space not only for parades and drill but also for sporting events such as this baseball game in front of the Long Barracks in about 1895. The Army encouraged participation in athletics as a wholesome way for soldiers to spend their spare time.

Quarters for the commander of the garrison on the Upper Post were built in 1888. Located at the northwest corner of the parade ground, they, like the commanding general's quarters on the Lower Post, provided an excellent view of the parade ground and the best exposure to the prevailing breezes. Brig. Gen. Joseph W. Stilwell lived here in 1940. The building was named the Stilwell House in 1959.

20

Looking west from the second story of the Long Barracks, this view shows the north and west sides of the Upper Post, including, from right to left, the band barracks, the company-grade officer quarters, the commanding officer quarters, and the west-side officer quarters. Behind the commanding officer quarters, the clock tower in the Quadrangle is visible.

At the entrance to the Upper Post was the first building to serve as the post headquarters. Designed by Alfred Giles and built in 1886, this building held the offices for the post commander and his staff as well as a court-martial room. Note the soldiers on the porch wearing the white trousers and helmets authorized for wear in the Southwest.

This view of the Upper Post from the clock tower in about 1890 shows the rear of the officer quarters along the north and northwest sides of the Upper Post parade ground. When flush toilets were installed in these quarters around 1900, the small buildings behind the quarters were converted from outhouses to servant quarters.

By 1892, about the time this photograph was taken, all 12 barracks and the sally port on the Upper Post were completed. This view shows the northeast corner of the parade ground, the sally port, and most of the other barracks. At the time, Fort Sam Houston was the second largest post in the United States.

In the center of the line of barracks on the Upper Post stood a sally port with the barracks above it originally intended for the band. The band was moved into a separate barracks in 1893, and this section was converted into a guardhouse. Here, guard mount is being conducted. The sentinels detailed from among the units in the garrison include both infantrymen (with rifles) and cavalrymen (with carbines).

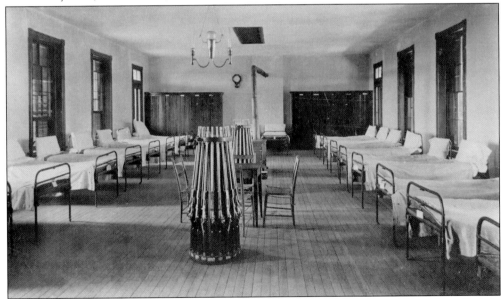

Each barracks had two sleeping bays like this one upstairs with a capacity of 20 soldiers. Built-in lockers at the ends of the bay held the soldiers' uniforms and gear. Rifles were kept in racks between the rows of bunks. The barracks are austere by modern standards but were a vast improvement over the facilities at the small frontier posts.

This guard mount on the Upper Post parade was accompanied by the band at left. The purpose of the guard mount was to inspect the sentinels going on duty to insure their readiness for that duty. After the inspection, the sentinels going off duty would be relieved, the new sentinels would be posted, and the remainder of the guard detail would be marched to the guardhouse.

In 1893, this purpose-built band barracks was constructed at the northwestern end of the line of barracks. A practice hall, offices, and noncommissioned officer rooms were on the ground floor. Upstairs was a dormitory for the bandsmen. The belvedere covered a platform where the band could play. The building was converted to administrative uses during World War I.

Between 1891 and 1893, one hospital steward quarters and four duplex noncommissioned officer (NCO) quarters were built behind the north end of the Long Barracks, seen here in the background. These were the first permanent NCO quarters built on the post. The duplexes were usually occupied by regimental and post staff NCOs. The hospital steward's quarters had a room set aside as a dispensary.

Post Q.M. Sgt. Michael Mullen poses with his wife and family in 1888 at his quarters on the Upper Post. With Mrs. Mullen are, from left to right, their children Alice, Mary, Dick, and Florence. The post quartermaster sergeant managed the receipt, storage, and issue of supplies for the garrison of the post.

Daddy Bowen

The noncommissioned officers of Light Battery F, 3rd Artillery, pose on the steps of the barracks on November 19, 1893. Often referred to as a cavalry post, Fort Sam Houston usually had a mixed garrison of all arms, with cavalry, infantry, and artillery. "Daddy Bowen," second from the right, is Sgt. Benjamin F. Bowen.

Cpl. John W. Buerkle, Company G, 23rd Infantry, stands on the porch of the Upper Post barracks around 1894 with his "trapdoor" Springfield rifle. His uniform and equipment, particularly the white gloves, suggest that he is prepared for parade or formal guard mount. Corporal Buerkle would remain in the 23rd Infantry until he retired in 1911 as the regimental color sergeant.

In 1891, this consolidated mess hall was built behind the Upper Post barracks. It was designed to feed the entire 12-company garrison during mealtimes. In 1906, company mess halls were built for each barracks, and this building was converted into a post exchange and gymnasium. The gym included gymnastics equipment, bowling lanes, and a shooting gallery.

On the firing line about three miles north of the Upper Post, firers engage targets at a range of 600 yards during the 1888 Department of Texas marksmanship competition. They are using the "Texas position," favored for long-range shooting. This parcel of land, purchased in 1886, would be separated from the post by ranch land until 1917, when the land in between was purchased by the Army.

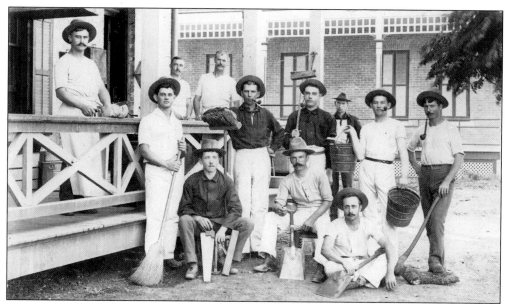

Behind one of the wing barracks, soldiers from Light Battery F, 3rd Artillery, take a break from their fatigue details. Their duties can be surmised from their tools: the soldier on the porch is a cook, the straw broom signifies kitchen police, the saw identifies the battery carpenter, and the shovels and push broom are for stable detail.

During the Spanish-American War, the 1st Texas Volunteer Cavalry, one troop of which is seen here, was mobilized at Fort Sam Houston to replace the Regular Army garrison, which was on its way overseas. These troops served at Fort Sam Houston and along the Mexican border for the duration. Here, they are equipped with the Pattern of 1860 Light Cavalry Saber and the 1879 Prairie Belt.

Two

THE LARGEST ARMY POST 1899–1916

Quarters No. 3 on the Lower Post, one of the field-grade quarters, were occupied by Col. Sidney W. Taylor and his family in 1902 while he was serving as adjutant general in the Headquarters, Department of Texas. During the expansion of the post after 1905, this neighborhood became known as the Staff Post.

Bessie Taylor, center, the wife of Col. Sidney W. Taylor, stands with her daughter and son-in-law, Bess and Max Graham, and two officers identified only as Rich and Doyl. Bess Graham holds her dog, Thirsty. Behind them is the combined officers' mess hall and bachelor officer quarters. Lt. Dwight D. Eisenhower would meet his future wife, Mamie Doud, on the porch of that building in 1915.

This view to the southwest from the belvedere of the band barracks shows, from left to right, two officer quarters, the officers mess/bachelor officer quarters, the post headquarters, and four more officer quarters. The street between the officers' mess and the post headquarters is the main entrance into the Upper Post. The gazebo on the parade ground served as a bandstand.

Department of Texas commander Brig. Gen. Jesse M. Lee (seated, center) sits with the officers of his staff in the Quadrangle in 1904. Seated to Lee's left is the chief paymaster, Maj. John L. Bullis. A veteran of the Civil War, Major Bullis had been the leader of the Seminole-Negro Scouts of the 24th Infantry Regiment during the Indian Wars.

A hospital steward (far right) leads a group of Hospital Corps privates in the conduct of litter drill in front of the post hospital. The privates are wearing their aid bags as well as slings to support the weight of the litters. The "casualties" on the litters are also Hospital Corps privates who will take their turn carrying the litters.

A sentinel armed with an M1903 Springfield rifle stands guard at the entrance to the Upper Post while an officer approaches. The building at the left is the bachelor officer quarters where Lt. Dwight D. Eisenhower lived in 1915. The other building is the post headquarters. Note the speed limit sign to the right.

For this full-dress guard mount in 1909 in front of the Long Barracks, the garrison has turned out a detail of more than 60 sentinels. In the right foreground stands a battalion sergeant major with his sword drawn. In the rear are the first sergeants of the companies providing the sentinels and the supernumeraries who stand ready to replace any sentinel failing the inspection.

32

This Nic Tengg postcard shows the northwest corner of the Upper Post before 1907. The entrance to the Infantry Post is to the left of the flagpole. The commanding officer quarters can be seen to the right of the largest water tank. To the left of these quarters are the gazebo and the clock tower.

Members of M Company, 9th Infantry, assigned to the post firefighting detail pose with their equipment on the Infantry Post. The two soldiers holding fire axes are wearing the blue denim fatigue uniform. The post would not have a full-time fire department until World War I. This image is from a postcard postmarked May 12, 1908.

Riflemen at the Leon Springs Military Reservation fire their M1903 Springfield rifles. Because the smokeless-powder M1892 Krag-Jorgensen rifle and the M1903 Springfield rifle could not be safely fired on post, the War Department had begun purchasing land in 1906 near Leon Springs, about 20 miles from the post, for field training and firing ranges. In 1917, this training area would be named Camp Bullis.

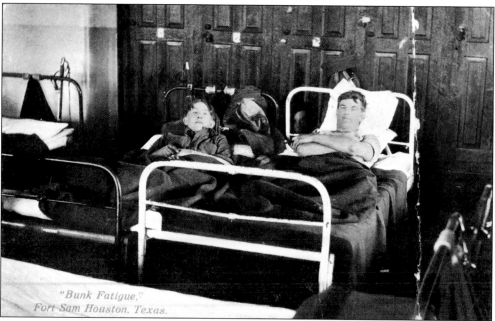

"Bunk Fatigue,"
Fort Sam Houston, Texas.

Two cavalrymen, identified as such by the cavalry sabers at the heads of the bunks, perform what was known by the soldiers as "bunk fatigue" in the barracks around 1905. The bunks are of the 1893 pattern. The built-in lockers in the background hold the soldiers' uniforms and equipment. With the construction of the Cavalry and Artillery Posts after 1905, this neighborhood was called the Infantry Post.

Members of the 6th Battery, Field Artillery, pose on the front porch of their new barracks on the Artillery Post in about 1905. This is the same unit as Light Battery F, 3rd Artillery, renumbered in a reorganization of the Artillery in 1901. Standing at the left in the first row is Benjamin Bowen, who by that time had risen to the rank of first sergeant.

In 1908, this 84-bed Station Hospital was built behind the Cavalry and Light Artillery Post officer quarters to accommodate the expanding garrison. The hospital area was conceived as a unitary neighborhood that included the hospital, barracks for the enlisted men, quarters for the hospital stewards, and quarters for nurses. Wings would be added to the building in 1910, increasing its capacity to 152 beds.

Company G, 9th Infantry, poses for a unit photograph at their barracks on the Infantry Post in December 1908. The company commander, identified as a captain by the three trefoils on the cuffs of his coat, sits front and center with his sword, while the first sergeant sits to his right. The numbers are keyed to a roster of the unit penned on the reverse of the photograph.

The Liscum Bowl commemorates the service of the 9th Infantry during the China Relief Expedition in 1900. Named for the regimental commander, Col. Emerson Liscum, who was killed in action at the battle of Tientsin, the bowl and 52 cups were made from a 90-pound block of melted silver, a gift to the regiment from the Imperial Chinese government for protecting a mint that was under attack.

These two views of a field artillery section allow a comparison of uniform and equipment changes. In both photographs, the cannoneers are operating the M1902 field gun. This quick-firing gun was the Army's first breech-loading gun with a hydro-spring recoil system. It could fire a three-inch shell of either high explosive or shrapnel by indirect fire to a range of 8,500 yards. To the left is the ammunition caisson. In the upper photograph, from about 1905, the crewmen wear dark blue pullover shirts and cotton breeches and campaign hats creased fore-and-aft. They are wearing M1903 pistol and cartridge belts and carrying .38-caliber Colt revolvers in their holsters. In the lower photograph, taken in 1909 at Leon Springs, the campaign hats are in the Montana peak style, and the shirts are olive drab flannel.

Cavalrymen from the 3rd Cavalry conduct a "skirmish run" on the Staff Post. In this drill, the troopers are training to fight dismounted, using their rifles rather than their sabers. In accordance with US cavalry doctrine, the units used their horses to move rapidly about the battlefield but dismounted to fight.

A trooper from the 3rd Cavalry conducts a drill called "Running at Heads." The trooper canters along a path and engages a series of targets mounted on posts using his revolver and saber. Head posts are engaged with the revolver or saber cuts. At ring posts, the object is to run the point of the saber through a metal ring four inches in diameter.

Members of the 3rd Cavalry Regiment, clad in padded vests and helmets and armed with wooden practice sabers, conduct mounted fencing practice. The original owner of this postcard identified the officer under the "x" as the commander of the 3rd Cavalry Regiment, Col. James Parker, who was known as "Jumping Jim."

On October 17, 1909, Pres. William Howard Taft presided over the ceremony for the dedication of the new post chapel. Built with funds donated by the citizens of San Antonio and the members of the garrison, it is known as the Gift Chapel. The officer behind the president is his military aide, Maj. Archibald Butt. Three years later, Major Butt was lost at sea when the RMS *Titanic* sank.

The entire garrison of Fort Sam Houston—the 3rd Cavalry, the 3rd Field Artillery, and the 9th Infantry—turned out for the dedication of the new post chapel in October 1909 by Pres. William Howard Taft. Prior to this, there was no chapel on the post, so Chaplain Thomas Dickson started a campaign to raise funds for the construction of a chapel. About $50,000 was raised. Architect

Leo M.J. Dielmann of San Antonio designed the chapel in neoclassical style, with modified Corinthian columns at the entrance and a copper Roman-style dome. Mayor Bryan Callaghan of San Antonio, Secretary of War Jacob M. Dickinson, and Dielmann attended the ceremony. President Taft dedicated the edifice "to peace, good will, and humanity."

"ARTILLERY INSPECTION, U.S.A."

A light artillery battery is drawn up for inspection in front of the cavalry barracks in about 1906. In this postcard, the four guns of the battery are positioned behind the far end of the formation, and ammunition caissons are behind the near end. From October 1900 onward, a battalion of two such batteries has been in the garrison.

Prepare to mount

Soldiers from the 3rd Field Artillery conduct crew drills with their M1902 field guns on the Artillery Post. Crewmen take turns performing the duties at each crew position. Behind them at left is one of the latrines. These were the first troop latrines on the post with flush toilets. At the right is one of the two-company mess halls.

42

This postcard was based on a George Bain photograph taken between 1904 and 1907. The whole garrison of Fort Sam Houston—an infantry regiment, a cavalry regiment, an artillery battalion, and the band—are formed up on the Lower Post for a grand review. This area would soon be referred to as the Staff Post.

The 22nd Infantry Regimental Band poses with its instruments in 1911 in front of its practice hall and barracks on the Infantry Post. The bandsmen are wearing the Pattern of 1902 dress uniform. The bandmaster stands at the far left. The commanding officer of the band stands at the far right.

Pioneer aviator Benjamin Foulois waves to the camera. A plumber in civilian life, Foulois enlisted during Spanish-American War, transferred to the Infantry, and was commissioned. He transferred into the Signal Corps, and after limited instruction by the Wright brothers, he was ordered to take Signal Corps Aircraft No. 1 to Texas and "teach yourself how to fly." This he accomplished on March 2, 1910, at Fort Sam Houston.

In February 1910, the Army paid Otto P. Kroeger and Company $1,450 to construct this aeroplane shed on the cavalry drill ground to house Signal Corps No. 1, the Army's only airplane. The pyramidal frame structure in front of the hangar was the catapult, which was required to launch the plane.

Signal Corps Aircraft No. 1 sits in front of its hangar at Fort Sam Houston in May 1910. Two members of the Signal Corps Aviation Detachment, Felix Clark and most likely William Bailey, pose in the aircraft. The Signal Corps insignia can be seen on the rear stabilizer. The wheels are not landing gear; they were for moving the aircraft around on the ground.

Lieutenant Foulois gained fame as a pioneer aviator, but his enlisted men were needed to made it all happen, including, from left to right, (seated) Pfc. Felix G. Clark, Sgt. Stephen J. Idzorek, Pfc. Bert C. Brown, Pfc. Vernon L. Burge, and Sgt. Herbert R. Marcuse; (standing) Oliver Simmons, Pfc. Bruce C. Pierce, Pvt. Glenn R. Madole, Pfc. Kenneth L. Kintzell, Pfc. Roy J. Hart, and Cook WIlliam C. Abolin. Not shown are Master Signal Electrician Charles Chadburn, Pfc. Edward Eldard, and Pvt. Berkeley Hyde.

Army officers examine a Wright biplane during the 1911 Maneuver Camp at Fort Sam Houston. At the controls is Phillip Parmalee, an instructor pilot employed by the Wright brothers. This aircraft was one of several used by the Army in experiments to determine what practical use could be made of aircraft.

Soldiers from the 17th Infantry Regiment from Fort McPherson, Georgia, stand by one of the unit's Colt-Maxim M1904 water-cooled machine guns at the Maneuver Camp. Shown here is the equipment of a machine gun platoon, including the two guns, the water cans, the ammunition basic load, tools, spare parts, and packsaddles.

Soldiers from the 18th Infantry march along one of the trails at the Leon Springs Military Reservation during the 1911 Maneuver Camp. During this period, brigade- and division-sized maneuvers were conducted on and around the reservation. In these maneuvers, the Maneuver Division faced an "enemy" composed of other units detached from the division.

The Regular Army and the militia occasionally trained together. At the 1911 Maneuver Camp, militia officers were ordered to perform their annual training and were attached to the different regiments of the Maneuver Division. These officers served with the 18th Infantry Regiment. Officers from the National Guards of Texas, New York, and Pennsylvania can be identified by their collar insignias in this group.

Pr camp at Ft. Sam Houston, S. A. Tex.

21

Above, a battalion of the 10th Infantry Regiment forms up for a review during the Maneuver Camp at Fort Sam Houston in 1911. Below, the same battalion of the 10th Infantry is formed up for a review and seen from a slightly different angle. Note the box on the ground in front of the formation and the very tall sergeant at the end of the first rank of troops. These similarities indicate it is the same formation. Below, however, a Wright Model B aircraft appears to be flying over the formation. Despite the novelty of aircraft at the time and its low altitude, not one of the soldiers is paying attention to the plane, indicating that the plane may have been added to the original image.

Flight operations resumed at Fort Sam Houston in 1916. The Aviation Post was established on the land acquired in 1886 for a rifle range and campground. The L-shaped building beyond the rows of tents was the troop barracks. The two buildings to the right are the hangars, each capable of housing five biplanes. There were no runways, only a level grass field for takeoffs and landing.

Lt. Dwight D. Eisenhower and his wife, Mamie, stand on the steps at St. Louis College in San Antonio. Lieutenant Eisenhower, on his first of two tours at Fort Sam Houston, was detailed to coach the St. Louis College football team by Maj. Gen. Fredrick Funston, the Southern Department commander. St. Louis College would become St. Mary's University in 1927.

INTERIOR OF
QUADRANGLE

This 1916 view of the interior of the Quadrangle shows that it lost some of its scenic appearance during the mobilization of the National Guard. The amount of material that had to pass through the depot required the construction of additional office space in the form of a two-story building to the left of the clock tower to manage the depot operations. Eventually, almost a million square

feet of space had to be rented in San Antonio to handle the volume of supplies. This would eventually lead to the construction of new depot facilities outside the Quadrangle. Note the new clock in the tower, the deer in front of the water tank on the right, and the mixture of horses and horseless carriages.

Following Pancho Villa's raid on Columbus, New Mexico, in 1916, Camp Wilson was established at Fort Sam Houston for the training of many of the 100,000 National Guardsmen mobilized for border service. Set up on the drill grounds northeast of the Cavalry Post, the tents could accommodate some 10,000 troops. The Gift Chapel and clock tower are visible along the skyline.

Soldiers from the 3rd Field Artillery fall out in front of their barracks for the daily retreat ceremony. This event marks the official end of the soldiers' day. The bugler sounds "Retreat," the soldiers salute, and a cannon is fired. The bugler then plays "To the Colors" as the American flag is lowered from the post flagpole.

Three

THE WAR TO END ALL WARS AND THE PEACETIME ARMY 1917–1927

When Camp Travis, named for William Barrett Travis, defender of the Alamo, was built in 1917, this complex housed the headquarters of the 90th Division. This division began assembling and training in July 1917, shortly after construction of the cantonment was completed. After its training was completed, the 90th Division shipped out to France and was replaced here by the 18th Division.

This typical two-story barracks could accommodate 200 men. The one-story portion on the right end was occupied by the company kitchen. The ground floor was used in part for the soldiers' bunks and for the dining room, which also doubled as the classroom. Just two stoves heated this entire 11,180-square-foot building. Providing illumination were 61 electric light fixtures.

To handle the burgeoning number of troops pouring into Camp Travis and the other posts in the San Antonio area for training, the War Department leased 15,427 acres of land south of the 17,274-acre Leon Springs Military Reservation. The building in the right foreground was the headquarters for this installation, soon named Camp Bullis. In modified form, this building is still the camp headquarters.

A squad of recent recruits from the 90th Division practices the manual of arms with obsolete Krag-Jorgensen rifles in November 1917 because the division had only just begun to receive the new M1917 rifles in October. The bayonets for the rifles can be seen stuck into the ground near each soldier's feet.

An officer from the 315th Engineer Regiment inspects the construction of field fortifications near the unit barracks at Camp Travis. Engineers could also build bridges and clear obstacles. The 315th was part of the 90th Division, the "Tough 'Ombres," which had begun training at Camp Travis in July 1917 and was deployed to France in June 1918.

In May 1917, a remount station moved its headquarters into this building, the former Aviation Post headquarters. A remount station received, trained, and issued horses and mules to the cavalry, artillery, and other units, which needed draft or riding animals. Staffed in part by former cowboys and even polo players, this remount station processed more than 200,000 horses during the war.

The two buildings that had served as hangars on the Aviation Post were converted to warehouses for the remount station when flight operations moved to Kelly Field in May 1917. During World War II, these buildings served as dining facilities for the units being mobilized and trained in the adjacent tent camp. The former hangars were demolished in 1960 to make room for an Army Reserve center.

The band from one of the battalions of black soldiers in the 165th Depot Brigade at Camp Travis poses at YMCA No. 1. The Depot Brigade received, examined, and processed inducted soldiers and forwarded them to the units in which they would serve. Most of the black inductees were assigned to service-type units. The Army fielded few black combat arms units during this war.

Members of the Telegraph Section of Company D, 51st Telegraph Battalion, stand on the steps of the former artillery band barracks. These Signal Corps soldiers wear khaki cotton trousers, olive drab flannel shirts, black silk ties, and campaign hats. Their chief, third from the left in the front row, wears the chevrons of a sergeant first class, Signal Corps.

Fire Station No. 1 was the headquarters for the Camp Travis Fire Department. With more than 1,400 wooden buildings, Camp Travis needed a robust fire service. Fire Truck and Hose Company 412 manned the several fire stations and observation towers throughout the cantonment. The firefighters were soldiers assigned to the company.

A pair of Harley Davidson V-twin motorcycles from the 1657th Pigeon Section, 7th Service Company, Signal Corps, stand by on the service road near one of the Cavalry and Light Artillery Post mess halls in 1918. A Signal Corps lieutenant rides in the side car while a sergeant first class tows the trailer.

BROOKS FIELD AMBULANCE AIRPLANE - JN 4 D - LANDING ON PARADE GROUND,
FORT SAM HOUSTON, TEXAS, SEPTEMBER 12, 1918.

A Curtiss JN-4 "Jenny" biplane lands in front of the regimental headquarters building on the Cavalry Post parade ground in 1918. The aircraft is marked with a red cross because it is being used as an ambulance in an experiment to see if aircraft could be used to transport battlefield casualties. This aircraft, from an Air Service squadron from Brooks Field in southeast San Antonio, has been modified by the addition of a compartment behind the pilot's cockpit. The top of the compartment is hinged so that it can be opened to allow a litter patient to be placed aboard the aircraft for transport. By the time of the Korean War, aeromedical evacuation was becoming routine.

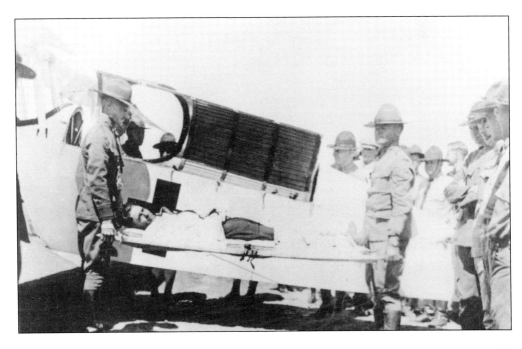

During World War I, the Army again rented buildings in San Antonio for the storage of supplies. This building at 1203 East Houston Street, near the present-day Amtrak Station, was previously occupied by the San Antonio Machine and Supply Company. In 1917, the Army rented it as Warehouse 20. It was involved in the reclamation of damaged material or equipment being returned from overseas.

Efforts to spruce up the drab Camp Travis cantonment area took hold in the postwar environment. Here, landscaping featuring military insignia and painted rocks brightens up the area by the barracks of the Headquarters Company of the 2nd Division. This division had just returned from overseas in 1919 and had taken station at Fort Sam Houston.

On November 27, 1925, the soldiers of the 2nd Division turned out for a photograph opportunity. The soldiers were arranged on the Cavalry Post to form the 2nd Division's shoulder sleeve insignia, with the men wearing different color shirts forming the various design elements. The division commander, Brig. Gen. Paul Malone, is at the point at the bottom of the formation.

THE SECOND DIVISION, U.S.ARMY
BRIG. GEN. PAUL B. MALONE
COMMANDING
NOVEMBER 27, 1925
DESIGN: LT. F.X. DORN
© G.F. Jennings.

When the neighborhood east of the Quadrangle was cleared away for the construction of new warehouses, only this building was spared. Built and operated as Krause's Meat Market, it was converted into the meat branch of the Quartermaster Retail Store. Here, military families could purchase meat and meat products at reduced prices. It was the forerunner of the military commissary sales stores.

This aerial view shows the new warehouse complex of the San Antonio General Depot in 1931. More than 600,000 square feet of storage space was now available to the depot. At the bottom of the photograph is the Infantry Post. At the top is the Gift Chapel and some of the buildings of the New Post. During World War II, the depot would expand again.

Fort Sam Houston, Texas. Oct. 16, 1921.

A female visitor to the Quadrangle poses for a photograph on a Sunday afternoon in 1921 while other visitors stroll the grounds. At the base of the tower is a bronze plaque bearing President Lincoln's Gettysburg Address. This plaque would later be mounted inside the sally port on the wall on the east side.

A peacock strolls along the roadway in the southeast corner of the Quadrangle. The reason for the peacocks' introduction into the Quadrangle remains a mystery, but they have been there since at least 1898. The grounds of the Quadrangle, soon to be devoid of supply wagons, blacksmith shops, and the hustle and bustle of supply operations, underwent a series of beautification efforts after World War I.

As a swan glides gracefully around the pond, signs sternly warn visitors of the Army's concern for the welfare of the denizens of the Quadrangle. Beyond the pond, the deer, geese, and peafowl can be seen grazing. At this time, the population of the deer herd had reached about 40.

Though dedicated by President Taft in 1909 and accepted in 1911, the Gift Chapel was still far from complete in 1920. Columns like those at the Infantry Post were erected, but the driveway was unpaved and not landscaped. The saloons in the neighborhood across the street, many with "amusement rooms" with lewd women, had been demolished when the land was purchased for new warehouses for the Quartermaster Depot.

Between 1929 and 1938, the congregation of the Gift Chapel mounted several efforts to beautify the chapel. Stained-glass windows and fanlights were installed, as well as carpeting and new altar furnishings. A pipe organ and piano were also installed. Flags of the units that had served at the post were displayed above the pews from the balconies.

The primary function of this guardhouse, built in 1911 on the Cavalry Post, was to serve as the guard force headquarters. It was the sergeant of the guard's command post and the barracks for the off-duty sentinels. Its secondary purpose was a jail. In the basement were cells for minor offenders and soldiers awaiting trial.

The post bakery made bread and other baked goods for the units on the post. It also sold food to military families. Since 1915, the post bakery also operated the Bakers and Cooks School for the Quartermaster Department, training cooks, bakers, and mess officers. Lt. Dwight D. Eisenhower was a graduate of the Bakers and Cooks School at Fort Sam Houston.

A director confers with an American soldier playing the role of a German machine-gunner during the filming of King Vidor's World War I epic film, *The Big Parade*, released in 1925. Battle scenes were shot at Camp Bullis, and Fort Sam Houston provided the troops for the veritable "cast of thousands." The machine gun is a water-cooled Browning M1917.

The noncommissioned officer quarters at the east end of the Cavalry Post underwent a change after the war. During the war, the Army began to create a series of ranks between those of enlisted men and commissioned officers—warrant officers. Within the units at Fort Sam Houston, there were several warrant officers, including the bandmasters. The former NCO quarters were thus designated as warrant officer quarters.

The Station Hospital had its porches screened to reduce the risk of insect-borne disease. Notice the evacuation slide on the side of the building. Though 19 temporary wards had been added to the Station Hospital, this facility was still too small to adequately serve the number of troops on the post after World War I.

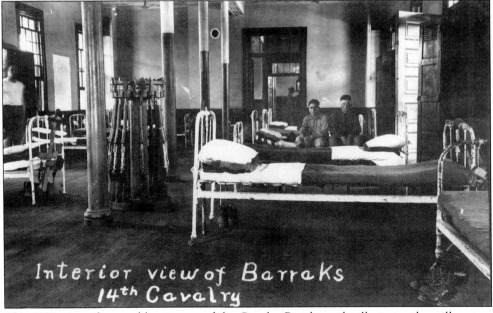

This 1920 view of a squad bay in one of the Cavalry Post barracks illustrates the still-austere furnishings—single bunks, lockers, and a weapons rack. The arms rack contains M1911 Colt automatic pistols and M1903 Springfield rifles. At the foot of each bunk is the cavalryman's M1913 saber. The bugle at the far left identifies that bunk as belonging to the troop bugler.

Members of Troop E, 14th Cavalry, sit down in the dining room of their mess hall on the Cavalry Post in 1920. Behind its barracks, each cavalry troop had its own latrine as well as a kitchen and a dining room in a building it shared with another troop. Dining room orderlies delivered platters of food to the troopers sitting at each of the tables.

On the parade ground in front of the barracks, the regimental commander, with his tie tucked into his shirt, conducts a full field inspection of troopers from the 14th Cavalry. Each item of the soldiers' individual equipment—haversack, cartridge belt, shelter tent, saddle, etc.—is laid out so the inspecting officer can check its completeness and serviceability.

The first sergeant (right) of Troop D, 14th Cavalry, and a corporal sit at a field table to take a meal in the field. In the background, other men of the troop pass through the field kitchen with their mess gear. The presence of the portable typewriter next to the corporal likely indicates that he is the unit clerk.

Most of the officer quarters for the Cavalry and Artillery Post were single-family units. The exceptions were the two four-family units like this one on the Cavalry Post. The four two-bedroom apartments included a parlor, kitchen, dining room, den, bathroom, and servant's room and were arranged two-over-two with a central stairwell. A similar unit was on the Artillery Post.

The Aviation Post resumed flight operations in 1925 and was designated as Dodd Field in 1928 for pioneer aviator Townsend F. Dodd. In this view, the airfield headquarters can be seen at the base of the water tank. Along the road to the right are the officer quarters. To the upper right of the water tank are the barracks and hangars. In the foreground is the post cemetery.

A mounted soldier poses near the crucifix in Mervale, a faux village built for the movie *Wings*. In the filming of this movie, the War Department loaned Paramount Pictures several thousand soldiers as well as tanks, aircraft, and the use of the Leon Springs Military Reservation. In all, troops from Fort Sam Houston were used in three major films in the 1920s, *Wings*, *The Big Parade*, and *The Rough Riders*.

Four

New Post and the Big War
1928–1947

When the 2nd Division returned from France to Fort Sam Houston, it occupied the facilities of Camp Travis. To accommodate the married soldiers in the division, some of the barracks and hospital wards were converted to family quarters, like these in the Soissons Area, seen here in 1923. Intended to last only seven years, these temporary buildings rapidly deteriorated, and their abysmal condition prompted Congress to act.

The first buildings completed in the New Post were the 9th Infantry Regiment barracks complex. Unit integrity was promoted, as the entire unit was housed together. The regimental headquarters and the service units were quartered in the building facing the parade ground. Each of the regiment's battalions occupied one of the other three buildings. The four buildings enclosed a small drill ground.

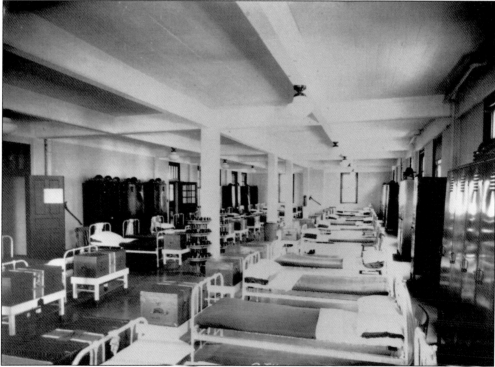

This squad room in the 9th Infantry Barracks illustrates the living conditions of the soldiers in the 1930s. The soldiers' uniforms and equipment are stored in the wall lockers and footlockers. The footlockers are color-coded to identify the soldier's unit. The bunks are the M1905 model. This is probably a squad room for the headquarters or service company, because the weapons racks contain only pistols.

Bemedaled marksmen from the Company D, 9th Infantry, rifle team pose on the steps of the back porch of the new 9th Infantry Barracks on the New Post with their M1903 Springfield rifles and their trophies in about 1935. They are wearing shooting coats over their khaki uniforms, along with campaign hats, wrap leggings, and high-top service shoes.

The barracks for the 15th Field Artillery included a center headquarters and service battery barracks and a wing for each of the two battalions containing the firing batteries. One legend about Fort Sam Houston is that horses were kept in the basement of these buildings. In fact, the horses were kept in the stables at the lower right. During World War II, these barracks were converted to hospital wards.

"A place for everything and everything in its place" aptly describes this field artillery tool room. On the shelves are the tools carried on each of the unit vehicles. The cabinets contain the tools of the maintenance section. This type of display facilitated property accountability and made an inspector's job easier. All of the cabinets and shelves were locally fabricated, indicating a high level of craftsmanship in the unit.

This 1935 aerial view shows most of the New Post. The officer quarters, with the commanding general's quarters at the bend in the parade ground, lie at the lower left of the photograph. On the opposite side of the parade ground, starting at the lower right, are the theater, the 9th Infantry Barracks, the post exchange, and the 15th Field Artillery Barracks. Along the top of the photograph are the NCO quarters.

Parked in front of the new post exchange (PX), the Budweiser Clydesdales deliver a wagonload of beer. The PX was part of a cluster of community facilities. Next-door were a cafeteria and a service station. Though later enlarged, this building would serve as the PX until 1972, when it was replaced by a much larger facility.

Inside this quartermaster warehouse was the sales commissary. This view shows the arrangement of the groceries on the shelves. The post newspaper described this as the "Piggly Wiggly style" after the grocery chain of that name, the first truly self-service grocery store. This type contrasts with most grocery stores at the time, because the groceries were readily accessible to the customers.

The New Post also included the new Station Hospital. Completed in 1937, the hospital had a 418-bed capacity. It would develop into a general hospital and be designated as Brooke General Hospital in 1942. It was named for Brig. Gen. Roger Brooke, a distinguished medical officer who had commanded the old Station Hospital at Fort Sam Houston from 1929 to 1933.

Urban planning concepts configured the New Post as a series of unitary neighborhoods. All the elements of the Station Hospital were in one neighborhood. This aerial view of the hospital complex shows, from left to right, the nurses' quarters, the hospital, and the enlisted medical detachment barracks. To the left, out of the picture, was a cluster of family housing units for the medical officers assigned to the hospital.

76

The main entrance to the hospital building was the most ornate exterior element in the New Post. Flanking the caduceus, the Latin inscription reads, "Dedicated not to Us but solely to the Health of Mankind." Under this porte cochere, vehicles delivered ambulatory patents, hospital staff, and visitors. The hospital would expand to a general hospital in 1942 and form the core of Brooke Army Medical Center in 1947.

An ornately appointed lobby greeted visitors to the new Station Hospital. The floor was covered with colorful tile, and the ceiling, doors, chairs, and even the woodwork at the information desk were ornately carved. Seen here in 1941, the lobby was featured in a scene from the Warner Bros. short subject *Soldiers in White*.

Brig. Gen. George C. Beach, seen here at his desk in the new Station Hospital headquarters, served as the commander of the hospital as it expanded during the 1940 mobilization through the end of World War II. In the 1941 short film *Soldiers in White*, produced by Warner Bros. and shot at Fort Sam Houston, General Beach had a bit part playing the role of hospital commander.

The neighborhood containing the officer quarters of the New Post, built between 1931 and 1934, faced the barracks from across the parade ground. Bungalows for field-grade officers lined the edge of the parade ground, while the more numerous two-story company-grade quarters were set back. At the bend in the parade ground were the quarters for a general officer, seen here at the far left.

The two-story officer quarters of the New Post were the most common type of officer quarters. Variety was provided by alternating arched and squared entryways and by reversing the floor plans. These three-bedroom homes included a kitchen, a dining room, a living room, and two bathrooms. They were also the last family quarters at Fort Sam Houston to include a servant's room.

With the entire 23rd Infantry Regiment formed up on the Infantry Post parade ground on September 3, 1937, a company passes in review. Most of the soldiers are armed with the M1903 rifles with bayonets, but near the left flank of the formation, four men are armed with pistols, and one in the rear rank is armed with the Browning Automatic Rifle.

Two styles of buildings were used on the 150 noncommissioned officer quarters built in the New Post. To add variety to the neighborhood, the styles were alternated along the same side of the street, as seen in both of these images from along Chaffee Road. As the photographs illustrate, the quarters on the opposite side of the street from each other were also alternated, so any set of quarters faced a set of the other style. Below, Quarters 826, at the left edge of the photograph, has a gable roof and rounded arches on the front porch. It faced Quarters 827, above at the right edge of the photograph, with a hip roof and squared arches on the porch. Both photographs show the two roof styles and porch details side by side.

These state-of-the-art (for 1930) radios and telephone switchboards equipped the Eighth Corps Area communications center in the northwest portion of the Quadrangle. From here, the headquarters could communicate with the units and installations in the five-state corps area and with the War Department in Washington. The communication center is staffed by soldiers and civil servants.

Here, four soldiers from the 23rd Infantry Regiment get haircuts, a shave, and a shoeshine. This barbershop was located in the basement of the Infantry Post gymnasium, which had been built in 1891 as the consolidated mess hall. In the other sections of the post, most company-sized units had their own barber and tailor shops.

This new theater was completed in 1935. Built during the era of movie palaces, the theater was lavishly decorated in Spanish Colonial Revival style, as it was intended to be the "ace theatre" of the Army motion-picture circuit. Built at a cost of $139,213.74, the theater was richly decorated inside and out with cast stonework, decorative tile, and ornate woodwork.

This is the view from the balcony, where the general's box of reserved seats was located. The frescoes flanking the screen show the Mission Concepcion (left) and Mission San Jose, both of which are in San Antonio. The ornate fixture in the ceiling is the vent for the air-conditioning system. The theater's capacity was 1,201.

A machine gun crew from Company M, 9th Infantry Regiment, trains at Camp Bullis with the Browning M1917A1 heavy machine gun. The sergeant on the left wears the newer herringbone twill field uniform. The soldier on the right wears the older blue denim fatigues. Both are wearing the "Daisy May" field hat.

Sgt. Maj. Jimmy Brought (right) of the 12th Field Artillery chows down with St. Louis Cardinals baseball star and former 12th Field Artillery soldier Jerome "Dizzy" Dean. Sergeant Major Brought, a recipient of the Silver Star Medal for heroism in World War I, coached and pitched for the 12th Field Artillery's baseball team. It was Brought who recruited Dean into the 12th Field Artillery and gave him his nickname.

Actor Robert Young, best known for his role in *Father Knows Best*, attended the grand opening of this building, the Officers' Club, in 1935. Young was in town for the premiere of the movie *West Point of the Air*, which was being filmed at Randolph Field. The Officers' Club included a dining room, a dance patio, several card rooms, and a swimming pool, as well as several apartments.

Lt. Gen. Herbert Brees, the commander of the Eighth Corps Area, hosts a group of Latin American officers at a dinner in the Officers' Club on October 7, 1940. The main dining room is decorated with the guidons of units in the 2nd Division. Commands at Fort Sam Houston have had a long-standing tradition of exchange visits with Latin American armies.

84

From 1934 to 1937, the US Coast Guard operated from Dodd Field with a squadron of planes that included this Curtiss Falcon O-11. The Coast Guard was supporting the US Customs Service in the suppression of the smuggling of alcohol, illegal aliens, and drugs. This squadron was the last aviation unit to use Dodd Field before it was converted into a recruit training camp.

Troop A, 1st Armored Car Squadron, from the 1st Cavalry Division at Fort Bliss, came to Fort Sam Houston in September 1937 to participate with the 2nd Division in the Provisional Infantry Division Tests. These T11-series armored cars performed reconnaissance duties for the division. Barely visible at the far end of the row of T11 vehicles is a T2E2 LaSalle armored car.

The corporal (second from left) leads this scout car section from the 23rd Infantry Regiment. During tests, the Army often provided nonstandard vehicles to substitute for unavailable types. This sedan gave good on-road mobility but very limited off-road mobility and no armor protection. The section's armament, the Browning Automatic Rifle (BAR), can be inferred from the BAR magazine belts that three of the soldiers are wearing.

Crewmen dismount from the M2A2 light tanks of the 2nd Tank Company during a demonstration of the tanks on the parade ground. The crewmen are wearing coveralls and tanker helmets, which protected their heads while bouncing around inside the vehicles. The twin turrets of these newly arrived armored vehicles led to them being nicknamed "Mae Wests."

On the reviewing stand for the 2nd Division parade during the 1940 Fiesta de San Antonio on April 22 are, from left to right, Maj. Gen. Walter Krueger, commander of troops; Lt. Gen. Herbert Brees, commander of the Eighth Corps Area and serving as the reviewing officer; and Harry Jersig, who was named King Antonio XXII. Since the first Fiesta de San Antonio in 1891, the Army's participation has been an important feature.

The decor in the library in the commanding officer quarters on the Infantry Post reflects the occupant's previous service in China. Brig. Gen. Joseph W. "Vinegar Joe" Stilwell lived here from 1939 to 1940 while serving as the commander of the 2nd Division's 3rd Infantry Brigade. He would later command American troops in the China-Burma-India theater during the war. These quarters were designated as the Stilwell House in 1959.

Brig. Gen. John Lucas (center) poses with Maj. Maxwell Taylor (left), Sgt. Maj. Harry Roberson, and Pat, a horse in the 12th Field Artillery. Pat was retired in 1938 when the 12th Field Artillery was motorized, living in retirement until his death in 1953 at the age of 45 years. Major Taylor would later serve as Army chief of staff and chairman of the Joint Chiefs of Staff.

This photograph, taken after the Provisional Division Tests from the top of the general hospital looking south, shows the 2nd Division draw up into its three regimental teams with their supporting elements. At the front of the formation stand Maj. Gen. Walter Krueger and the 2nd Division staff. This type of organization, dubbed the "triangular division," was adopted for all of the Army's infantry divisions.

In 1940 and 1941, some 500 mobilization buildings like this barracks were built at Fort Sam Houston as part of the Emergency Construction Program. These robust, austere structures, which could be built with a minimum of skilled labor, housed the rapidly expanding Army. Often referred to as "World War II temporaries," most were in fact constructed before the United States entered the war.

The interior of this barracks for the 52nd Signal Battalion is typical of those throughout the post and around the nation. This squad bay is filled beyond its normal capacity, with bunks filling the center aisle. The large metal cans mounted on the columns are "butt cans." The level of the water in these cans for extinguishing cigarettes was prescribed in the post regulations.

Infantrymen from the 2nd Division prepare to load a 37mm M3 Antitank Gun into a mock-up of a transport plane in July 1941. Using trials like this, the 2nd Division determined which items of equipment in the division could be airlifted to the battlefield. From this, the table of organization and equipment of an airborne division was developed.

Soldiers from the 9th Infantry Regiment load an M3 Antitank Gun into a Douglas DC-2 aircraft from the San Antonio Air Depot at Kelly Field during airborne division tests in July 1941. The tests culminated in 1942 with an exercise where the 2nd Division conducted an air assault to seize the airport at Brackettville, Texas.

Three C-47 transport aircraft are parked on the parade ground near the service club. They had landed on the parade ground towing CG-4 Waco gliders to familiarize the troops of the 2nd Division who would be riding them on the air assault to Brackettville and to the maneuvers in North Carolina.

Troops gather around for a close-up look at one of the gliders flown in to Fort Sam Houston. Before the Brackettville operation, the troops loaded up into the gliders for a familiarization flight and took off from the parade ground. These tests helped validate the concept of an airborne division.

Second Division soldiers take to the firing ranges. In the right foreground, they fire the Browning Automatic Rifle. In the left background, they fire the M1 rifle. Both groups are using the coach-and-pupil method, where the soldier firing is the pupil and the other man coaches the pupil's technique and makes corrections. The soldier on the field telephone is talking to the pit detail marking the targets and recording the scores.

On December 17, 1942, members of the 30th Women's Army Auxiliary Corps (WAAC) Post Headquarters Company arrived by train from Fort Des Moines for service at Fort Sam Houston. This all-female unit was the first of its type to be deployed for service, replacing men in administrative jobs in garrisons to free up manpower for service overseas.

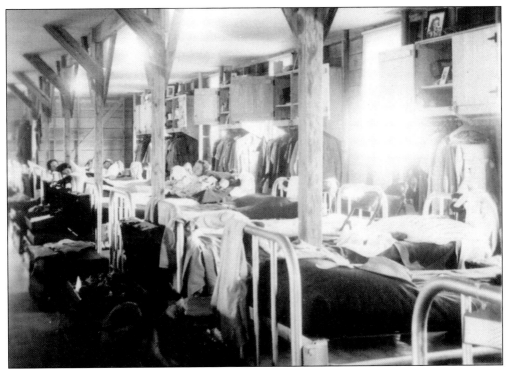

The barracks occupied by the WAACs were similar to those occupied by the men but included a beauty shop and laundry facilities. The beds appear to be hospital beds rather than Army bunks. Here, the barracks have a lived-in look. Rather than wall lockers, the women had their uniforms hanging on a rack below wall-mounted cabinets.

In contrast to the previous view of the WAAC barracks, here the women and the barracks are standing tall for an inspection. Each WAAC stands by her bunk with her footlocker open for inspection. The contents of the footlocker were prescribed in detail, as was the manner of their stowage in the footlocker.

This group of recent recruits marches along Winans Road along the south edge of the War Department Personnel Center at Dodd Field in 1943. They are wearing the olive drab herringbone twill uniforms, helmet liners, and canvas leggings. These troops had been students at Texas Agricultural and Mechanical College (Texas A&M) who enlisted in the Army en masse.

Two lieutenants from Company F, 38th Infantry Regiment, adjust the sights on a Browning Automatic Rifle in 1941. This weapon served as the base of fire in infantry squads and platoons. The 38th Infantry had recently been transferred to the 2nd Division from Fort Douglas, Utah, and was quartered in the New Post and in the mobilization temporaries.

94

Military police trainees armed with M1903 Springfield rifles run an obstacle course at Fort Sam Houston in 1942. The Provost Marshal General School was established here to train military police officers and enlisted men and to mobilize military police units. The Military Police Corps was established as a branch of the Army in 1941.

M.Sgt. Marinius "Max" Bronkhorst served as an instructor in judo and the use of the bayonet during World War II. Here, he demonstrates the jab with his M1903 Springfield rifle and bayonet. Master Sergeant Bronkhorst had been the noncommissioned officer in charge of the Signal Corps pigeon lofts on post and was a nationally renowned pigeon racer.

A mortar section from H Company, 3rd Battalion, 9th Infantry poses in its weapons carrier. In the bed of the truck is an 81mm mortar. The crew members hold an M1903 rifle, a Colt M1911 pistol, and an M1918A2 Browning Automatic Rifle. This mortar, with a range of 3,300 yards, provided indirect fire to support the battalion.

Configured as a "triangular division," the 2nd Division was well endowed with motor vehicles. Lined up for a division review are, from the lower left to the upper right, the 2nd Medical Battalion, the 2nd Quartermaster Company, an artillery battalion, and an infantry regiment. Though the division had been equipped with the new M2 howitzers, the troops are still wearing the M1917A1 helmets.

Vehicles from the Headquarters Company, 3rd Battalion, 9th Infantry, parade along Houston Street through downtown San Antonio in 1942. In the front is the Antitank Platoon in quarter-ton utility vehicles known as "jeeps," towing the 37mm M3 Antitank Gun. These soldiers are wearing the M1 steel helmet and the M1941 field jacket.

Trucks from Battery B, 37th Field Artillery, tow their guns as they approach the Alamo on Army Day, April 4, 1942. The howitzers are the 105mm M2. This type of howitzer, recommended by the Westerveldt Board, remained in use until after the Vietnam War. As the artillerymen in the trucks had not yet been issued the M1 steel helmet, they wear the M1917A1 helmet.

Enlisted men from the Headquarters Company, Fourth Army, pose at the Infantry Post sally port. Fourth Army Headquarters had moved from the Presidio of Monterey, California, to Fort Sam Houston in January 1944 to take over the responsibility for mobilizing and training Army forces in the western half of the continental United States.

As a result of the change in Fort Sam Houston's mission, the Medical Field Service School from Carlisle Barracks, Pennsylvania, moved to Fort Sam Houston. The school occupied the former 9th Infantry Barracks. Within this quadrangle, the school had its classrooms, billets for its students, a dining facility, and an officers' club annex known as "The Pit." The school stayed in this quadrangle until 1972.

Five

HOME OF ARMY MEDICINE AND MORE 1948–1976

Soldiers from Company A, 1st Battalion, US Army Medical Field Service School (MFSS), pass in review during a retreat parade. These soldiers are wearing the "jacket, field, wool," popularly known as the "Ike Jacket," and the garrison cap. Though the Army was not officially desegregated until 1948, the companies of the MFSS were integrated.

After World War II, the shortage of family housing was so acute that the Infantry Post barracks, shown here on October 8, 1948, with the porches enclosed, was considered for conversion into apartments. This action was not undertaken, and when the Korean War broke out in 1950, the Infantry Post barracks were converted into a reception station instead.

To accommodate the increased number of married personnel at Fort Sam Houston as a result of its change in mission, many of the mobilization temporary buildings were converted into apartments. A typical barracks, like these seen in October 1948, could be converted into three officer apartments or five noncommissioned officer apartments.

Pvt. Paul Brochan stands by the Company D, 2nd Battalion, barracks in 1951. Private Brochan, a trainee at the Medical Field Service School, wears the olive drab herringbone twill fatigues and brown two-buckle combat boots. The MFSS trained the officers of the Army Medical Department—doctors, nurses, veterinarians, and pharmacists—the officers of the Medical Service Corps, and enlisted medical specialists.

The Medical Replacement Training Center (MRTC) operated in the complex of mobilization temporary buildings east of the New Post's noncommissioned officer quarters. The MRTC conducted advanced individual training for the enlisted medics. Some of the field training, such as litter drill, was conducted in the wooded area in the upper right of this photograph. This aerial view was taken on January 29, 1952.

Pfc. Milburn Gable, Company A, 307th Military Police Battalion, plays taps on the bugle at the Fort Sam Houston National Cemetery on May 26, 1952. Private First Class Gable is wearing the cotton khaki uniform with the service cap and white military police accoutrements. The cemetery was first established as the post cemetery in 1926 but was redesignated as a national cemetery in 1937.

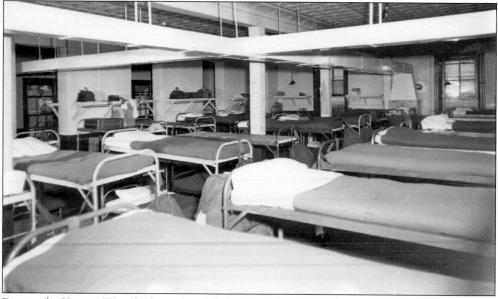

During the Korean War, the barracks of the Infantry Post housed an induction center, receiving draftees and recalled former service members, known as "retreads." The inductees' stay here was short. After in-processing, they were shipped to basic training, to service schools, or to existing units. Note that these 1880s-built barracks still retain their original pressed-tin ceilings.

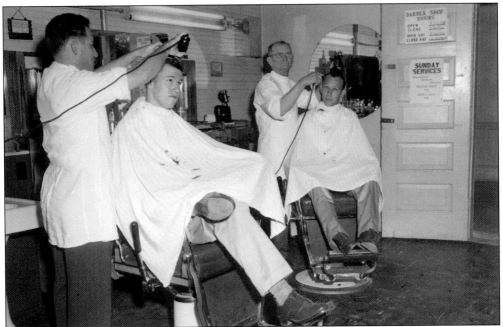

At the induction center on the Infantry Post, these recently arrived soldiers-to-be get a GI haircut as part of their in-processing. The inductees would also be examined by medical personnel to determine their fitness to serve, would be tested to determine their aptitude for the various jobs in the Army, and would receive their uniforms.

In their new uniforms and fresh haircuts, soldiers at the induction center pass through the chow line for breakfast in June 1952. The soldier on the right is a cook wearing the traditional "cook's whites." The compartmented trays simplified the process of feeding large numbers of troops by reducing the number of items that had to be cleaned afterwards.

New inductees shop at a branch post exchange on the Infantry Post in June 1952. The post exchange stocked toiletries, snack foods, cigarettes, and other items the trainees would need during their short stay. The main post exchange stocked a wider selection of consumer goods at lower prices than civilian department stores.

Their induction complete, these troops are ready to be shipped out to basic training, to units, or to service schools at other posts around the country. On their collars are two discs bearing the letters US. After completing advanced training, they would wear the insignia of their assigned branch on the left side of the collar and the US disc on the right.

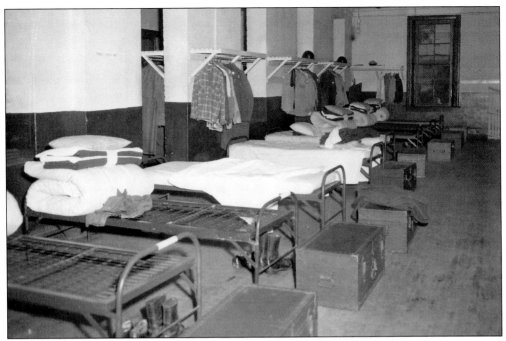

With the truce that suspended hostilities in the Korean War, the number of troops passing through the reception center decreased. Double-decking the bunks was no longer necessary. The soldiers' uniforms were hung on a bar rather than in lockers. What appear to be the doorways in the walls are actually the original barracks windows, which were opened up when the porches were enclosed in 1939.

These barracks on the Cavalry Post were for the personnel in the deployable units assigned to post rather than for trainees. The bunks are better than those in the reception center, and each soldier has a wall locker and a footlocker for his clothing. The soldiers' field gear was stored on top of the wall lockers, and their weapons were stored in an arms room in the basement.

By way of contrast, this photograph shows a room for two female soldiers in the Artillery Post. As there are only two people in this room, the occupants are probably noncommissioned officers. They have footlockers and a rack for their uniforms and civilian clothing, but also a dresser, a lamp, and bedspreads rather than blankets. The stuffed animals are strictly nonregulation.

Retired Maj. Gen. Benjamin Foulois, former pilot of Signal Corps Aircraft No. 1 and chief of the Air Service from 1931 to 1935, salutes as Fort Sam Houston troops pass in review. This ceremony, on March 2, 1955, commemorated the anniversary of the birth of military aviation in 1910 with the erection of a monument near the post flagpole.

In 1955, the Army transferred the US Modern Pentathlon Training Center from West Point to Fort Sam Houston. Here, the groom, R. Garza (left), and stable sergeant, Sfc. H.W. Smith, work in the pentathlon stables with horses Patrick and Breeze. The center trained the US National Team for international and Olympic competitions. Pentathlon events included cross-country running, marksmanship, fencing, swimming, and horseback riding.

One of the perks of being a three-star general at Fort Sam Houston is that you get to have your picture taken with pretty girls during the annual Fiesta de San Antonio. Here, Lt. Gen. Isaac D. White, Fourth Army commander, poses with four young ladies who will be riding on the Army floats in the several parades conducted as part of the Fiesta.

After World War II, medical training became the mission of the post and a larger proportion of soldiers were married, creating an increased need for family quarters. To fill part of this need, these 24 "quadruplexes" were constructed on the Infantry Post parade ground in 1948. This aerial view shows the Infantry Post in 1957.

Explosive ordnance disposal technicians Cpl. William Roach (left), Sfc. Irvin Nichols, and Sfc. Franklin Mitchell (right), from the 137th Ordnance Detachment, check the device that will detonate an unexploded 81mm mortar shell on April 25, 1960. All three are wearing the cotton sateen fatigues introduced in the 1950s and the "Ridgway"-style cap. Behind them is their M38-series "truck, utility, one quarter ton," or jeep.

This aerial view shows the north end of the post in 1953. From the foreground back is the Fort Sam Houston National Cemetery, the facilities used by the reserve components, and Watkins Terrace, the first Wherry housing development at the post. At the lower right, to the left of the bend in the road, is the section of the cemetery set aside for the graves of the 144 Axis prisoners of war.

Trainees at the US Army Medical Training Center receive a class in gastric suction from a cadre master sergeant. After the Korean War, this school was established at Fort Sam Houston to provide advanced individual training to enlisted medical personnel. This class is being presented in one of the mobilization temporary buildings in 1961.

Members of the 312th Logistics Command, an Army Reserve unit from San Antonio, participate in a command post exercise at Camp Bullis on August 8, 1961, during their annual training. This unit's mission was to coordinate the logistics in the rear area of a field army. Noted author, historian, and columnist T.R. Fehrenbach served in this unit.

Maj. Gen. Ralph Osborne, the deputy commanding general of the Fourth Army, troops the line in the Quadrangle on June 12, 1961, in a review honoring his assumption of duties in the Fourth Army headquarters. The Color Guard wears the abbreviated summer uniform, adopted in 1956. At this time, the Fourth Army commanded all Army installations within a five-state area.

At the Camp Bullis training area, about 20 miles north of the post, trainees from the US Army Medical Training Center carry a simulated casualty in 1964. The trainee at the right can be identified by his shoulder sleeve insignia as an Army Reservist and a member of the X Corps.

A cadre sergeant from the US Army Medical Training Center conduct a class on the types of land mines used by the Communist insurgent forces in South Vietnam. On the table are an antitank mine and two types of "Bouncing Betty" antipersonnel mines. This class was conducted at the Vietnam village in 1965.

In 1965, Fort Sam Houston constructed the RVN (Republic of Viet Nam) Village at Camp Bullis. This facility, intended to familiarize trainees with tactical situations and operations they might encounter in Vietnam, followed in the tradition of the North African village, the German village, and the bunker complex built at Camp Bullis during World War II to train soldiers for combat in those areas.

Maj. Gen. William A. Harris, the commander of Fort Sam Houston, and some of the cadre from the US Army Medical Training Center stand at the entrance to the Vietnam village at Camp Bullis in 1965. The soldier to General Harris's right wears the traditional "black pajamas" worn by peasants and Vietcong in Vietnam. The others wear the fatigue uniform. The subdued insignia was first authorized later in 1965.

Members of the 24th Evacuation Hospital stand ready behind the Infantry Post barracks for a final inspection during a mobility training exercise on May 6, 1966. The purpose of the exercise was to evaluate the unit's readiness for deployment overseas. In the summer of that year, the "24th Evac" would be serving in Vietnam.

Lt. Col. Alexander Pouska Jr. inspects the M14 rifle of Pvt. ? Bumpas of the 24th Evacuation Hospital while another lieutenant colonel from the "24th Evac" looks on during the mobility training exercise. Below his canteen on his left side, Private Bumpas is wearing the M17 protective mask in its carrier.

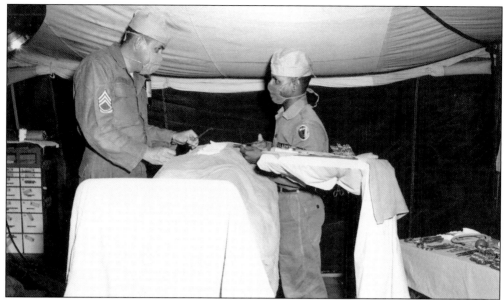

During their annual training at Camp Bullis in June 1967, Army Reservists Sfc. Pat Coffia (left) and Sp6c. Charles Brown from the 44th Evacuation Hospital from Oklahoma City simulate an operation on Pfc. ? Huddleston from the 47th Field Hospital. Reserve component units from all over the five-state Fourth Army area would come to Camp Bullis for their two weeks of "A.T."

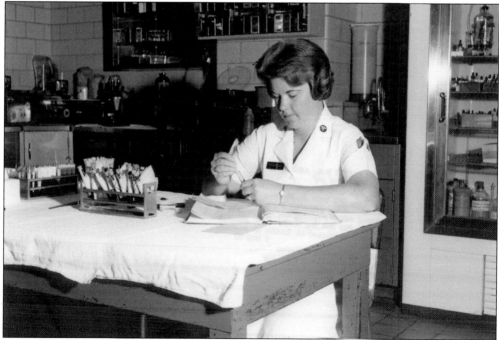

WAC lab technician S.Sgt. Neda Streepy prepares a blood sample for testing in the laboratory at Brooke Army Medical Center on May 2, 1967. In addition to serving as a full-service general hospital since 1942, this facility became an Army medical center in 1947, when it was put in charge of the Medical Field Service School, the Army Surgical Research Unit, the 67th Medical Group, and other medical activities.

In 1968, the Fort Sam Houston Military Museum was moved into the Stilwell House to save the building from demolition. Though the chain link fence added to the security of the building, it was very much out of place in the historic Victorian-era neighborhood. After the museum moved again in 1975, the building fell into disrepair.

The 2nd Division Room, one of several themed displays in the Fort Sam Houston Military Museum, contained artifacts and other materials relating to the 2nd Infantry Division, known as "Fort Sam Houston's Own." This room had been the library when the building served as family quarters. The other displays in the museum were the Fort Sam Houston Room and the Bataan Room.

Two developments of ranch-style family quarters, a mixture of duplexes and single-family houses, were built on the post to alleviate the housing shortage. The first, Watkins Terrace, was built at Dodd Field in 1951 for noncommissioned officers. This unit, a duplex built near the hospital in 1953, was part of Harris Heights, which housed junior officers.

The 323rd Army Band, with its members in the dress blue uniform, stands on the parade ground within the Medical Field Service School quadrangle in 1969. This quadrangle had previously been the 9th Infantry's barracks. The bandleader, a warrant officer, stands at the left, and the drum major, a sergeant first class, stands at the right.

Fort Sam Houston's parade float gets ready to participate in the Fiesta Flambeau parade in San Antonio on April 28, 1969. Miss Fort Sam Houston, Bettye Sue Mack, rides at the rear of the float. She is accompanied by princesses Pansy May Welch (left) and Marilyn Peters. Each of the major elements at the post sponsored a float and selected representatives to ride on it.

These Spartan open-bay barracks in one of the mobilization temporary barracks were due for a face-lift in 1971. Under the Volunteer Army, or "VOLAR," Program, these barracks of the 78th Engineer Company were partitioned into individual cubicles. The purpose of the VOLAR Program was to improve the living conditions of soldiers in order to retain them in service.

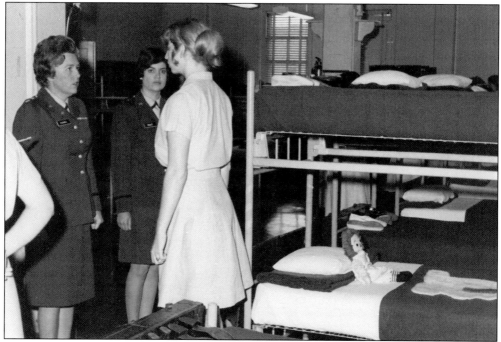

Maj. Nancy Russell, the commanding officer of the Women's Army Corps Detachment, Company D, US Army Medical Training Center, conducts an inspection of her troops as 2nd Lt. Judith Pruitt looks on. At the time of this photograph, in 1972, women were organized into WAC detachments and billeted separately from men. In 1978, the WAC was abolished as a separate corps, and women were assimilated into all but the combat branches of the Army.

Road guards are posted to allow this company of WAC medical trainees to safely cross the street as they march through the barracks area of the US Army Medical Training Center in 1973. These WACs are wearing the light blue physical training uniform with the garrison cap. Near the rear of the formation, in fatigues and a helmet liner, is a member of the school cadre.

Charles K. Boatner of the National Park Service (left) and Ralph Langley of the San Antonio Chamber of Commerce unveil the dedication plaque for the Fort Sam Houston National Historic Landmark during Veterans' Day ceremonies in 1976. The marker is located near the post flagpole in the New Post. Designation as a National Historic Landmark recognized Fort Sam Houston's contributions to the nation.

In 1973, the Medical Field Service School, which trained Army Medical Department officers and medical specialists, and the US Army Medical Training Center, which trained enlisted medics, were merged to form the Academy of Heath Sciences. For the academy, a new administration building (lower right) and a new classroom facility (center) were built on the New Post.

Four new barracks complexes and a dining facility were constructed for the enlisted medical trainees in 1972. One of the barracks was set aside for the female trainees. There was also a new bachelor officer quarters for the officers attending the Academy of Health Sciences. A large parking area was required, because by this time, most soldiers owned cars.

This room in the new barracks, belonging to a female soldier attending the Academy of Health Sciences in 1974, looks more like the room of a typical American 19-year-old than like a soldier's area in the barracks. There is nothing particularly military about the room's furnishings except the bed itself.

Following the designation of the post as a National Historic Landmark, more attention was paid to the maintenance of historic buildings. These Georgian Revival-style quarters on the Artillery Post were built in 1905 for officers. The ornate woodwork was expensive to maintain, but the landmark status meant it would no longer be neglected. (HABS.)

These quarters were built on the Cavalry Post in 1909 for company-grade officers. As the post grew and changed after World War I, these quarters were designated for the chief of staff of the Third Army, which had arrived at the post in 1933. In 1941, that position and these quarters were occupied by Brig. Gen. Dwight D. Eisenhower. (HABS.)

Many of the Artillery Post quarters retain their original interior details, like this built-in sideboard in the first-floor dining room, now painted off-white with a center inset shelf and leaded-glass cupboards on each side and above. The inset shelf is backed by three mirrored glass panels. The center panel is a movable pass-through opening from the pantry in the next room. (HABS.)

Behind the parlor in these Artillery Post company-grade officer quarters is the stairway leading to the second story and the attic. Upstairs are three bedrooms and the original bathroom plus an added bathroom. The door to the left leads to the added half-bath under the stairs. What had been the servant's room behind the kitchen has become a breakfast nook. (HABS.)

Supported by four mobilization temporary chapels and a permanent chapel near the Academy of Health Sciences, the Gift Chapel was the hub of religious activity on the post. Office space was provided for the chaplains and administrative staff in the wings of the chapel. Three chaplains who served here rose to the position of Army chief of chaplains: Cols. John Axton, Edmund Easterbrook, and Alva Brasted. (HABS.)

During Armed Forces Week in 1971, a chapel memorialization program was undertaken. Along the sides of the nave, the flags of the states and territories of the Union and the District of Columbia were displayed. Above the altar were the flags of the United States, the Army, Texas, and the City of San Antonio. These were flanked by the flags of the Army's corps and divisions that served here. (HABS.)

The Long Barracks continued to be used after the Korean War. It was used as a barracks for reserve component units on annual training and for barracks and office space during several large-scale command post exercises. During the Vietnam War, the Long Barracks was home for conscientious objectors during their modified basic training before their training to become medics. (HABS.)

The old post headquarters building had been converted into bachelor officer quarters in 1919 with duplex apartments. In 1941, it was further modified into two two-room apartments, each with its own bath, on each floor. In the 1970s, it was used as temporary quarters for officers or noncommissioned officers on temporary duty. (HABS.)

124

The Staff Post quarters continued their traditional role as the high-rent district at Fort Sam Houston. Most of the general officers on the post lived in this neighborhood, even though many were not part of the headquarters in the Quadrangle. Though this house was originally built for a company-grade officer, at this time, it was usually occupied by a colonel. (HABS.)

Even though medical training and medical treatment comprised the majority of activity at Fort Sam Houston, the senior officer was still the commander of the headquarters in the Quadrangle. Thus, that officer resided in the Pershing House. When this photograph was taken, Lt. Gen. William B. Caldwell III, the commanding general of the Fifth US Army, lived here. (HABS.)

This is the front sitting room on the southwest side of the commanding general's quarters. At left is the hexagonal tower at the south corner of the building. Ornate pocket doors separate the front living room from the dining area to the right. This segmental arch passageway is also decorated with ornamental carved openwork. (HABS.)

After 100 years on Government Hill, the clock tower in the Quadrangle has become a symbol of the Army's presence in San Antonio. Throughout that time, Fort Sam Houston has performed important service to the nation. The motto inscribed on the stone tablet below the clock has provided sound advice since that time and for the foreseeable future: "In Peace, Prepare for War." (HABS.)

ABOUT PRESERVATION FORT SAM HOUSTON

Preservation Fort Sam Houston, Inc., a 501(c)(3) private, nonprofit, educational organization not affiliated with the Department of Defense, was established in 1984 to serve as an advocate for historic preservation at Fort Sam Houston and to support the activities of the Fort Sam Houston Museum. The organization participates with Fort Sam Houston in the preservation process as an interested party in the local community. It has pioneered the concept of the public-private partnership for preservation projects on military installations. After obtaining an out-grant from the Army for the use of the dilapidated Stilwell House, the organization carried out a series of fundraising programs to renovate the building. The Army funded the required lead and asbestos abatement and installed a new standing-seam metal roof. By 1998, the Stilwell House had been restored to its previous grandeur. Preservation Fort Sam Houston held a grand reopening of the Stilwell House as a dual-use community facility available to military organizations at Fort Sam Houston for meetings and other official functions while also serving as the organization's headquarters and a venue for its meetings and special events. Preservation Fort Sam Houston has continued its efforts to promote historic preservation and to support the Fort Sam Houston Museum.

DISCOVER THOUSANDS OF LOCAL HISTORY BOOKS FEATURING MILLIONS OF VINTAGE IMAGES

Arcadia Publishing, the leading local history publisher in the United States, is committed to making history accessible and meaningful through publishing books that celebrate and preserve the heritage of America's people and places.

Find more books like this at
www.arcadiapublishing.com

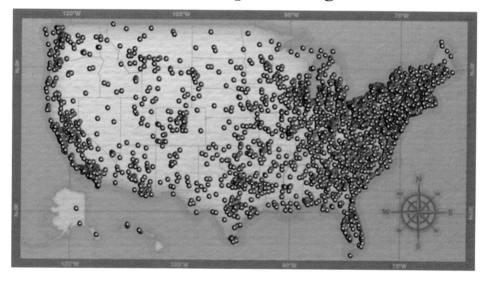

Search for your hometown history, your old stomping grounds, and even your favorite sports team.

Consistent with our mission to preserve history on a local level, this book was printed in South Carolina on American-made paper and manufactured entirely in the United States. Products carrying the accredited Forest Stewardship Council (FSC) label are printed on 100 percent FSC-certified paper.

MADE IN THE USA